Modern LOCOMOTIVES ILLUSTRATED
Annual No. 1

By Colin Marsden

The winter weather is often a bad time for railways in the UK, with timetables thrown into chaos at the first sign of snow. In the 2008-09 winter we saw several days of difficult travel conditions on most routes, especially those around London and the home counties when 6-8in of snow fell.

The UK rail network seems to have great difficulty in dealing with natural winter weather problems, with icing of the third rail and overhead power lines, frozen points, trains frozen in yards and staff unable to get to work. Let alone the difficult conditions on platforms, where little or no snow clearing was carried out on several main stations.

However, in other countries, notably Canada, Austria and Switzerland, the public transport networks operate like clockwork, the public daily grind is not drastically changed, buses operate (on time), schools remain open, roads are kept clear or gritted and trains operate.

Recent experiences in all three countries reveal that around 95 per cent of their passenger trains operate to time in heavy snow conditions. The 2009 winter in Canada was moderately bad as North American winters go, but the Canadian VIA network, not to mention local passenger services all kept running, some late operations were reported on the country wide services, but in the main everything ran. The public expected it to operate and rely on its timely operation.

In February 2009 I spent several days looking at, photographing and riding on Canada rail services in the Toronto-London-Windsor/Sarnia area, in that period we had heavy snow on several days, and temperatures well below freezing every day. The VIA operation was a true credit to the rail people of Canada, even on routes through the notorious snow belt from Toronto to London via Kitchener where

passenger services are few and accumulations of snow are common, services were never more than a few minutes down. What was even more surprising to a UK passenger, was that the full on-board services operated, meals for the Via1 or first class passenger and all serviced by a friendly and welcoming crew.

Sadly in the UK we just do not seem to be able to handle snow operations. The slightest trace of snow on the weather radar seems to indicate to Network Rail to issue blanket speed restrictions and even considering closure of some routes, while train operators issue temporary timetables with less trains, extended journey times and withdraw much of the on-board service.

In Canada as well as the principal countries affected by yearly snow in Continental Europe, specific snow clearing operations are planned, this might involve extra manpower to operate hand-operated clearing equipment, or the deployment of heavy duty snowploughs, these operate over the quiet night hours to ready the rail system for the peak passenger operations.

In the UK, Network Rail operate a fleet of snowploughs, but due to our limited falls of snow these tend to see little use. In fact some of the UKs fleet of 22 heavy duty drift ploughs, 10 Beilhack ex Class 40 ploughs and two snow blowers have never seen use.

In third rail electrified areas a small fleet of de-icing trains operate, scraping ice off the top surface of the live rail and applying an anti-freeze liquid, but frequently in the deepest of icy conditions, this is of little or no benefit as the icing causes serious electrical arcing with a risk of fire.

Snowploughs and rotary ploughs and snow blowers operate in most cold countries and

tend to keep rail networks open.

One of the benefits of the snowy conditions is the ability to photograph trains in the snow, in the UK these chances are grabbed by as many photographers as possible every time a fall occurs. In locations such as Canada, the opportunities are more plentiful and providing the roads are passable, which they usually are, even with more than a foot or more of loose snow, some wonderful images can be captured. The snow tends not to slow down the VIA operation and on many occasions photographers are left buried in snow blown up from a passing train, but the results are usually worth while. The one thing to always remember is to protect your camera, as even the top of the range models do not like too much water ingress.

With modern digital cameras the cold seems not to effect the working parts too much, unlike the days of equipment such as Pentax 6 x 7s which became very lethargic in cold conditions and frequently shot a frame at a slower speed than was required.

The old exposure compensatory values used by the non-digital cameramen still hold to some extend in todays digital world, but the complex automated metering and multi programme systems on the top of the range Nikon and Canon systems look after most exposure needs, especially if you are shooting in camera raw settings. ∎

With a temperature, including the wind chill down to around -25c photographers, especially those from the UK, tend not to want to stand around too much waiting for trains, or be in the spray area once the train goes by blowing up freshly fallen snow. This was the scene at the small town of Thorndale, mid-way between Stratford and London on 22 February 2009. Taken at 14.00, around 15min behind schedule, it shows train 85, the 11.00 Toronto to Sarnia via Kitchener traversing 'snowbelt' country. The three coach train is powered by snow laden General Motors F40PH2 No. 6413. This loco became something of a celebrity in the Canadian rail fraternity in winter 2009 as it powered the same two trains 85 and 88 every day from 2 February until 13 April. CJM

Above: The first few days of February 2009 will be remembered in London and the south for many years after heavy falls of snow put the rail system into chaos. However, the all important revenue earning aggregate traffic soon returned to near normal. On 3 February, Yeoman No. 59002 **Alan J Day,** *rounds the curve at Crofton on the Berks & Hants main line powering train 7A09, the 07.12 Merehead to Acton in a heavy snow storm.* **Bob Foster**

Below: The green of the Freightliner-livery stands out well against the snowy backdrop at Breich on the Edinburgh to Glasgow via Shotts line on 4 March 2009. The train, powered by Class 66/6 No. 66622, is the 6D62 the 07.54 Oxwellmains to Viewpark loaded cement tanks. **Fishbones Glover**

Above: The northern section of the UK, especially over Shap, and Beattock on the West Coast route frequently see snow in the winter months, but seldom falls in quantities that block the line and staff are more geared to deal with the problem. After a moderate fall, this was the view at Greenholme on Shap bank on 6 February 2009 with a Virgin Trains 'Pendolino' heading south with the 14.40 Glasgow Central to London Euston. Neil Gibson

Below: Visitors to the Gloucestershire & Warwickshire Railway diesel gala event on 6 April 2008 were treated to some unexpected overnight snow, which allowed some wonderful sun and snow images to be recorded. In superb light, Class 37 No. 37215 passes Hailes Bridge with the 10.00 Winchcombe to Toddington service. Martin Loader

Above: In conditions likely to see the UK railway cease normal running, Mainline Freight-liveried Class 60 No. 60011 passes Carstairs on 25 November 2005 while in charge of train 6S36 from Dalston to Grangemouth. Fishbones Glover

Below: Solid four-character route indicator box-fitted Class 40 No. 40195, painted in standard BR rail blue, passes through Mirfield in a slight glimmer of winter sun on 25 January 1984 following an overnight snow storm. The train is an empty oil from Leeds to the Stanlow oil refinery near Ellesmere Port. John Whiteley

Above: *The area around Basingstoke in Hampshire is not one where you would expect to find heavy snow, but over the years some moderate falls in this area have affected the smooth running of the railway. Here on 3 March 1981, rail blue-liveried Class 47/4 No. 47433 takes the Reading line away from Basingstoke with an early morning Poole to Manchester service.* CJM

Right: *Overnight snow and freezing conditions looked to have left their mark on these Eastern Region EMUs at Colchester on 14 January 1987. Class 308 No. 308137 awaits departure to London Liverpool Street, while an ice covered Class 312 passes on the main line.* Michael J. Collins

Left: *With a good covering of snow on the fells at Lambrigg, north of Oxenholme at lunchtime on 3 December 2008, the Network Rail New Measurement Train, formed of five recording cars, led by power car No. 43062, forms the 11.19 Glasgow Central to Crewe inspection train. The New Measurement Train spends around 60 per cent of its time working over the West Coast route ensuring near perfect conditions for the Virgin 'Pendolino' and 'Super Voyager' fleets.* Neil Gibson

West Coast Over the Fells

By Chris Perkins

The Lancaster & Carlisle Railway following several surveys to establish the best route north constructed the initial section of the West Coast Main Line over the fells from Lancaster to Carlisle. The line took it's current route due to the pressures of the inhabitants of Kendal who wanted access to this new form of transport, but this also added the extra climb of Grayrigg bank, the summit of which is just under 600ft above sea level.

The original plan was to tunnel under the summit at Shap to reduce the gradient, but much like current times there was an economic recession and the tunnel scheme was dropped as being too expensive, which resulted in the 4.5-mile climb at 1:75. The line is almost at sea level as it passes Hest Bank and in 34 miles climbs to 916ft at Shap summit.

When the contract for the line's construction was awarded, it was the biggest single railway contract since railway construction began and the line was completed in just over two years with through services to Carlisle commencing on 15 December 1846.

The route north from Carlisle was again the subject of various route surveys and opinion of the time felt that traffic levels would only support one Anglo Scottish route, with most favouring the East Coast route. In fact the North British Railway and the Newcastle & Berwick Company did build an East Coast route and once the bridge over the River Tweed was completed services between London and Edinburgh via Berwick commenced in October 1848.

However, as with the English section of the line, landowners in the Annandale Valley wanted the railway in their area and on 13 July 1845 the Caledonian Railway obtained an Act of Parliament to construct the line north from Carlisle to Carstairs where there would be a junction to serve both Edinburgh and Glasgow. This route followed the Annandale Valley before crossing over Beattock summit at 1,015ft then descending the Clyde Valley to Glasgow. The route terminated at Glasgow Buchanan Street for approximately 30 years until the current Glasgow Central station was opened in September 1879.

Although the northbound climb to the summit at Beattock was similar to that of Shap, it was just over twice the length with 10 miles of climb ranging from 1:74 to nothing less than 1:88. In fact apart from a few miles of downhill section in the Lockerbie area and a couple of other short sections it was a constant climb all the way from Gretna Junction. The southbound climb from Glasgow is not quite as steep but is virtually 50 miles of constant climbing.

The whole route was a very severe test both for locomotive designers and crews. All heavy trains in the steam era required banking with the bankers stationed at Oxenholme and Tebay for the Shap climb and Beattock for the climb to that incline. Even in the diesel era pairs of Class 50s were used in order to maintain the accelerated services to match the electric

services on the southern part of the route until electrification reached Glasgow in May 1974.

The diesel era came to the line at the start of the 1960s with mainly English Electric Type 4s taking over from steam on most of the workings which eventually did away with trains needing assistance.

To show how modern traction has dramatically improved the timings for services over the route, the start to stop timings between Preston and Carlisle for the fastest steam hauled service just prior to the Second World War in 1939 was 101 minutes, whereas today's Virgin Pendolino service covers the same distance in just 58 minutes - an incredible saving of 43 minutes for the 90 miles! At one time there were no less than 34 intermediate stations between Lancaster and Carstairs, on today's railway there are just four.

Despite some of the views having been spoilt by the overhead electrification structures and the building of the M6/M74 Motorways which parallel the line in places, if you like trains in big scenery, the route still offers some wonderful views either to enjoy from the train windows during a journey over the Fells or photographing the trains from the lineside.

Although traffic levels are not as high as they used to be, hopefully some of the following photographs showing the line today will demonstrate the wonderful images that can still be obtained of trains traversing the Fells. If you have not already made a visit, I hope they will tempt you to make the effort. ∎

Above: *Representing the final era before electrification, English Electric Type 4 No. 411 departs from Oxenholme station working the 11.32 Carlisle to Euston on 18 May 1971.* **J. H. Cooper-Smith**

Left: *GNER-liveried Class 90 No. 90024 represents the electrification era as it passes Crawford village in the Clyde Valley on the descent of Beattock with the 12.55 Carlisle to Millerhill Yard engineers train on 10 August 2005. This working is now diesel hauled and travels round the Edinburgh suburban lines instead of via Waverley station.* **Mark Bearton**

Below: *English Electric Type 4 No. D315 passes the classic location of Scout Green signal box on the climb to Shap summit with the 10.40 Euston to Carlisle in August 1964 in the immediate post steam era.* **M Pope**

Above: *With a dusting of snow on the Howgill Fells, Class 66 No. 66124 passes Docker with the 13.22 Carlisle Yard to Crewe Basford Hall engineers train on 24 January 2007.* **Mark Bearton**

Below: *A classic pairing of Class 50s over the Fells, showing Nos. 404 and 415 passing the loops south of Oxenholme on 18 May 1971 powering the southbound 'Royal Scot'. A Class 25 waits in the loop to head south with a freight off the Kendal branch. Due to engineering works, trains were being hand signalled by a flagman who can be seen at the side of the semaphore signal which has remained at danger.* **J. H. Cooper-Smith**

Bottom: *Class 50s Nos. 423 and 444 approach Oxenholme from the north with the 13.45 Glasgow Central to London Euston on 18 May 1971.* **J. H. Cooper-Smith**

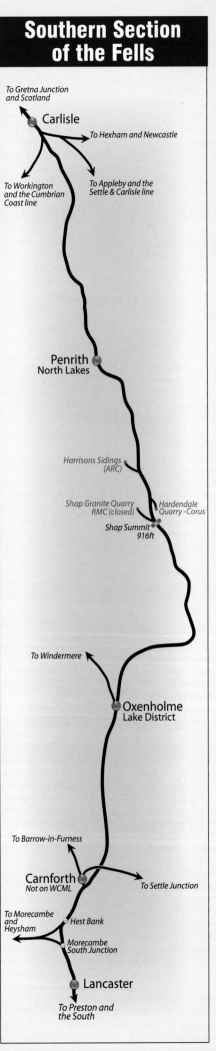

Southern Section of the Fells

To Gretna Junction and Scotland

Carlisle

To Hexham and Newcastle

To Workington and the Cumbrian Coast line

To Appleby and the Settle & Carlisle line

Penrith
North Lakes

Harrisons Sidings (ARC)

Shap Granite Quarry RMC (closed)

Hardendale Quarry - Corus

Shap Summit
916ft

To Windermere

Oxenholme
Lake District

To Barrow-in-Furness

Carnforth
Not on WCML

To Settle Junction

To Morecambe and Heysham

Hest Bank

Morecambe South Junction

Lancaster

To Preston and the South

Above: *With the Rosebud Willow Herb in full bloom Class 87 No.* 87016 **Willesden InterCity Depot**, *painted in InterCity-livery, heads north through the beautiful Lune Gorge leading the 14.35 London Euston to Glasgow Central on 7 August 1997.* **David Dockray**

Below: *Class 92 No.* 92022 **Charles Dickens** *heads a very lightly loaded 17.26 Carlisle to Eastleigh 'Enterprise' working downgrade at High Carlingill in the Lune Gorge north of Dillicar Common on 8 August 2003. The 1,240ft high Jeffery's Mount dominates the background.* **Neil Gibson**

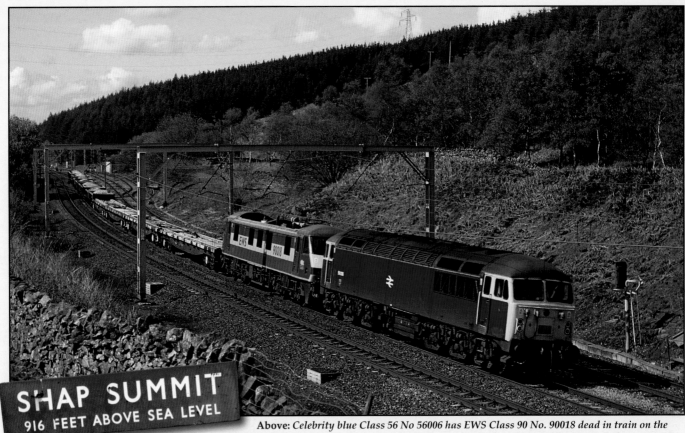

SHAP SUMMIT
916 FEET ABOVE SEA LEVEL

Above: *Celebrity blue Class 56 No 56006 has EWS Class 90 No. 90018 dead in train on the 6K05 Carlisle Yard to Crewe Basford Hall Yard engineers train passing the loops at Shap summit on 8 May 2003. The Class 90 had failed a couple of days earlier on the ECML and after being tripped to Carlisle it was being conveyed to Crewe for repairs. The formation had run the previous day but was stopped at Oxenholme with problems to the rails it was conveying and it returned to Carlisle.* **David Dockray**

Inset: *The Shap summit board, this particular board was replaced about two years ago but still reads the same.* **Jim Hocking**

Below: *English Electric Type 4 No. D267 heads uphill at Shap Wells on a London Euston to Perth service on 9 July 1960. The heavy train is made up of 14 coaches with a mixture of new Mk1s and ex-LMS designs, the photographer notes that the train was making steady progress and whilst unassisted was still making between 20 to 30mph.* **Tom Boustead**

Right Top: *Brand new BR Standard Sulzer Type 2 No. D5083 approaches Tebay from the south under clear signals at the head of a 15 coach test train. The Type 2 was reported over Shap bank as far as Penrith before returning south.* **Derek Cross**

Right Middle: *In the early days of dieselisation, the Glasgow Central to London Euston 'Royal Scot' service on 13 July 1963, glides downhill at Shap Wells powered by English Electric Type 4 No. D302.* **Jim Hocking**

Below: *Class 57/3 No. 57309 Brains has charge of the 10.25 Chirk to Carlisle empty log train as it climbs the last stretch to Shap Summit through the cutting on 8 May 2008. The loops at the summit are just to the left of the picture.* **Neil Gibson**

Above: *This picture demonstrates the topography that the builders of the railway faced in trying to cross the hills at Beattock. Class 390 'Pendolino' No. 390046 forms the 09.49 Glasgow Central to London Euston service on 3 May 2007, as it races downhill at Greskine.* **Chris Caley**

Below: *Freighliner Class 66 No. 66618* Railways Illustrated Annual Photographic Awards *heads downhill from Beattock summit at Greskine with the 14.07 Hunterston to Ferrybridge power station loaded coal working on 10 May 2006.* **Jim Binnie**

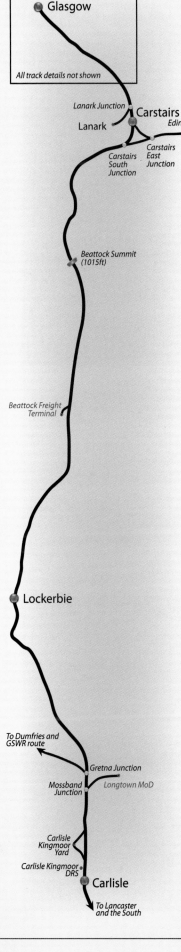

All track details not shown

- Glasgow
- Lanark Junction
- Carstairs
- Lanark
- To Edinburgh
- Carstairs South Junction
- Carstairs East Junction
- Beattock Summit (1015ft)
- Beattock Freight Terminal
- Lockerbie
- To Dumfries and GSWR route
- Gretna Junction
- Mossband Junction
- Longtown MoD
- Carlisle Kingmoor Yard
- Carlisle Kingmoor DRS
- Carlisle
- To Lancaster and the South

Beattock Summit
1016ft above sea level

← Glasgow 52 miles   **London →** 349 miles

Top: *A pair of English Electric Type 4s Nos. D445 and D412 breast the summit at Beattock and head downhill with a heavy 'Midland Scot' service on 1 August 1970.* **Derek Cross**

Above: *The summit board at Beattock loops, photographed in July 1973 when it replaced the original board which was attached to the signal box. The box can be seen in the background of the top picture.* **Chris Perkins**

Below: *Virgin Trains Pendolino No. 390027 sweeps round the curve at Abington loops forming a Glasgow Central to London Euston service on 23 November 2007.* **Fishbones Glover**

Above: *Virgin Cross Country Class 47 No. 47854* **Women's Royal Voluntary Service** *is seen substituting for an electric locomotive on 16 August 2001, as it heads the 10.31 Birmingham International to Edinburgh Waverley past Castle Hill.*
Scott Borthwick

Left Middle: *On 29 September 2005, EWS Class 66/0 No. 66044 climbs uphill approaching the River Clyde bridge at Crawford with a Hunterston to Fiddlers Ferry Power Station loaded coal working. The location of Castle Hill, also mentioned in other captions is located at the end of the tree line on the right of this view.*
Chris Perkins

Left Below: *Diverted from the East Coast Main Line due to engineering works, a GNER HST formation led by power car No. 43105 heads the 13.43 Edinburgh Waverley to Newcastle past Castle Hill on 3 September 2006. Power car No. 43114 is on the rear of the train.* **Jim Binnie**

Above: *Direct Rail Services Class 66/4 No. 66411 Eddie the Engine painted in Eddie Stobart livery crosses the iconic River Clyde bridge at Crawford with the Tesco Express from Daventry to Grangemouth on 4 March 2008. Jim Binnie*

Right: *Recreating a scene from the past preserved Class 50s Nos. 50028 and 50049 (operating as No. 50012) complete with Highland Stag motifs, pass Abington loops northbound with Pathfinder Tours 'The Orcadian' on 16 June 2006 from Swindon to Inverness. Jim Binnie*

Below: *One of the three 4-car tilting Voyager sets No. 221142 retained by Virgin Trains passes the snowy landscape of Little Gill north of Abington forming the 10.10 Glasgow Central to Birmingham New Street on 4 March 2008. Jim Binnie*

Electric to Shanklin

Above: *Ryde Pier is a double track railway but usually only one line is used. On 9 August 1989 4VEC No. 485041 heads towards Ryde Esplanade with a service bound for Shanklin.* **Peter Tandy**

Left: *After electrification the Island trains were frequently formed of seven car sets, one 4VEC and one 3TIS, but gradually these formations were reduced. With set No. 031 nearest the camera, a seven car train is seen at Sandown on 28 September 1977 bound for Shanklin.* **CJM**

The railway system on the Isle of Wight has long been noted for its unique practises and features and the use of old rolling stock. As part of the BR policy to replace steam traction with modern forms of propulsion, it was agreed in 1965 to modernise the Island rail system.

One option at the time was closure, but thankfully this was ruled out in favour of keeping one small 8.5 mile section between Ryde Pier Head and Shanklin open.

No suitable 'off the shelf' stock was available and 'new' trains were found in the form of retired 1927-design London Underground stock. These were fully refurbished at Wimbledon and formed into six three and six four car sets classified as 4VEC and 3TIS, derived from the Roman name for the Island.

The line from Ryde to Shanklin was electrified with the third rail (Southern Region) system at 630V dc. The first 'new' train arrived at a modernised Ryde depot in August 1966 and the new electric railway opened on 20 March 1967.

The VEC-TIS stock, painted originally in rail blue, was later painted in blue and grey and following transfer of the Southern Region to Network SouthEast in the mid 1980s the trains were outshopped in red, white and blue NSE colours.

By 1989 a major need for modernisation of the Island's rail system was again on the cards. With a reducing patronage and difficulties in finding more modern stock closure was again put forward. Thankfully this was not agreed and again London Underground came to the rescue, selling sufficient withdrawn 1938 tube vehicles to BR to form nine two-car sets classified 483, plus two spare vehicles.

These 'new' trains were refurbished at Eastleigh Works and commenced use on the Isle of Wight network in 1989. Originally sets were painted in NSE colours, but in 2000, following privatisation a decision was made to repaint sets in a blue livery with dinosaur branding.

In 2003 a start was made on repainting IOW sets into former London Underground red livery, with by 2009 most sets in this pleasing scheme.

Under privatisation the sets were owned by HSBC Rail, who agreed to sell the entire fleet to operators Stagecoach Rail for just £1 in March 2007. ∎

Map

Ryde Pier Head
Ryde Esplanade
Ryde St Johns Road
RY
Wootton
Smallbrook Junction
Havenstreet **X**
Ashey
Brading
Sandown **X**
Lake
Shanklin

Island Line
Double Track — Single Line

Isle of Wight Steam Railway
RY Ryde depot
X Single line passing point

©TRC 2009

Above: *The hub of Isle of Wight operations is Ryde St Johns Road, here the administrative headquarters of the railway is located, the depot, workshops and crew signing-on point. The signalbox on the country end of the 'up' platform now controls the entire Island line. Although colour light signalling is located at both ends of the system, the area around Ryde St Johns Road still retains upper quadrant semaphore signalling. With the 'down' signal off, VEC No. 485044 painted in NSE livery slows for the station stop at Ryde St Johns Road on 9 August 1989 formed of five vehicles.* **Peter Tandy**

Below: *With Ryde Pier usually operated as a single line from Ryde Esplanade, allowing the second track to operate as 'as required' with a 'shuttle' service along the pier, a cross-over just Ryde St Johns Road side of Ryde Esplanade station sees considerable use. A footbridge over the line linking the town with the hovercraft port provides an excellent view of operations, as witnessed by this illustration of 3TIS No. 486031 departing into Ryde Tunnel with a Ryde Pier Head to Shanklin service in the early evening of 11 August 1989. Much of the track ballast on the Isle of Wight uses sea shingle, which is not as robust as normal track ballast. The tunnel in the distance of this picture has a very restricted loading gauge and is the main reason that 'normal' stock cannot be used on the isolated network.* **Peter Tandy**

Left: *Carrying its Network SouthEast 'Ryde Rail' livery five-car formation No. 485043 departs from Ryde Esplanade station on 11 August 1989 with a train bound for Shanklin. Ryde Esplanade station is a good example of an easy to use passenger interchange with a bus station occupying the front of the station and a taxi rank adjacent. Public transport on the Isle of Wight is very popular with the near 2.5 million tourists who visit the resort every year. Few want the bother of taking cars to the Island and roads in places are very narrow and easily congested.*
Peter Tandy

Below: *A landmark day in Isle of Wight rail transport was on 13 July 1989 when the first of the 'new' Class 483 sets was put into passenger service. Network SouthEast, then under control of Chris Green, held a major media and press event on the line, showing the modernised railway to the local and national press. The July 1989 introduction of the new stock allowed a short time for enthusiasts to enjoy both 1927 and 1938-design stock to operate alongside each other. The first of the 'new' trains, set No. 001 is seen at Brading forming the 11.22 press special from Ryde.* CJM

Above: *To many railway purists, the 2000 repainting of Class 483 stock into light blue with dinosaur branding was almost too much to accept. Although an impressive use of modern stick-on graphics, the application did little to promote a quality rail operation. In Stagecoach branded dinosaur livery, set No. 006 approaches Ryde St Johns Road depot on 24 January 2003 with a service from Ryde Pier Head to Shanklin.* CJM

Below: *Adjacent to Ryde St Johns Road station is the line's depot and workshop. Over the years some outstanding work has been achieved at this site in keeping the two ageing fleets of EMUs available for traffic. Since its steam day use, the site has been fully modernised with two main two-vehicle length servicing roads, one has an elevated track and the other a deep inspection pit. Both lines are electrified using a 'trolley' system to alleviate the need for high voltage third rails inside the shed. Lifting jacks are provided on one road and a small workshop is situated next door. Set No. 004 is seen on track No. 1 on 23 March 2007, with a third rail shoe protection cover over the near pick up shoe and a door protection plate on the front, slid into position when sets are 'on shed' to avoid the possibility of a staff member trying to exit the cab from the front door.* CJM

Above: *Originally located at Waterloo East, and moved to Ryde St Johns in 1926, the signal box at the country end of Ryde St Johns Road station has controlled the entire Island rail network from 1989. The main view above shows the box in its 2008 condition with a metal stairway leading to the operating floor. In 2008 some 20 levers were still in use in the box. The inset view shows the operating floor in mid 2008. Both: CJM*

Right: *The driving cabs of the present Isle of Wight stock can best be described as 'basic' when compared with some of the hi-tech cabs used by fellow Stagecoach/South West Trains drivers on the mainland. This view of set No. 004, shows the main rotary power controller with a wooden knob on the right, the electro-pneumatic brake controller in the middle and brake, speed and indicator flags on the left. CJM*

Below: *In 2008 a launch was held at Ryde depot for the official introduction of the Isle of Wight railway as a Community Railway, with the first set re-launched in ex-London Transport style red livery, a little more traditional and pleasing than the dinosaur scheme it replaced. Set 004 is seen pulling out of No. 1 road at the depot on 18 January 2008. Throughout 2008 some major facelift work was carried out on remaining sets to improve their passenger accommodation, this included new seat moquette, lino and some wall coverings. An updated route map was incorporated and some advertising was installed at cant rail height. CJM*

Island Line Fleet List

1927 Design Stock
Booked formations
3-TIS Class 451

031	1 + 47 + 26
032	3 + 92 + 28
033	5 + 93 + 30
034	7 + 94 + 32
035	9 + 95 + 34
036	11 + 96 + 36

Spare Car 10

4-VEC Class 452

041	13 + 41 + 27 + 20
042	15 + 42 + 29 + 22
043	2 + 43 + 31 + 19
044	4 + 44 + 33 + 21
045	6 + 45 + 48 + 23
046	8 + 46 + 49 + 25

Due to maintenance needs, accident damage and vehicle condition, considerable mid formation of sets was reported.

1938 Design Stock
As delivered formations
Class 483

001	121 + 221
002	122 + 222
003	123 + 223
004	124 + 224
005	125 + 225
006	126 + 226
007	127 + 227
008	128 + 228
009	129 + 229

Many cross formations were soon recorded after introduction. Only six units remain operational.

Above: With the disused station buildings on the southbound side at Sandown behind the train, set No. 008 looking rather decrepit awaits the signal to enter the single line towards Shanklin on 18 January 2008. CJM

Right: One of the great pleasures of travelling on the present Isle of Wight railway system is that the original design air whistles as used on London Underground stock are still used. These are mounted on a bracket to the side of the drivers cab window and operated by a push button, allowing a main reservoir air supply to vent through the whistle. CJM

Below: The only passing place on the IOW network south of Ryde St Johns is Sandown, where the two train service is always booked to meet. On 21 March 2008, red set No. 009 pulls into the platform, while dinosaur liveried set No. 006 awaits a green light to head towards Ryde. Stacey Thew

Rails to Slovenia By Philip Wormald

The idyllic country of Slovenia is in Central Europe in the Eastern Alps. It borders the Adriatic Sea, between Austria and Croatia. Despite its small size, this Eastern Alpine country controls some of Europe's major transit routes.

The country broke free from Yugoslavia around 15 years ago and is now slowly being discovered as one of the most beautiful and tranquil countries in the world. There are vast subterranean caves, turquoise rivers, silver lakes, medieval castles and much more.

The Railways consist of a total of 1,201 km (746 miles) of standard gauge lines of which 499 km (310 miles) are electrified at 3000V DC. Virtually all routes offer great scenery and the trains are very comfortable. New orders have meant delivery of newer more modern standard types of locomotives and multiple units, but still some of the older types will remain for years to come. The 'stars' of the fleet for many railfans are the Class 664 *Reagan* diesels due to their incredible loud sound so if you make a visit, don't miss them, as with more electrification they may well be sold soon.

The Trains

Class 342

Forty of these Bo-Bo electric locomotives were built by ASGEN in Italy from 1968 for the then Yugoslavian Railways. After the break up of JŽ all the class remained with the Slovenian Railways. They were intended for smaller freight trains and the lighter weight passenger trains but even today the class can sometimes be found on quite heavy freight traffic.

In recent years some members of the class have been taken out of use and sold on to private operators in Italy. Both the FNM (Ferrovie Milano Nord) and FER (Ferrovie Emilia-Romagna) have taken delivery of some locos. FNM use theirs as Class E640, mostly on freight traffic, but also with some passenger trains between Milano Nord and Cadorna. The FER only use their locos on freight traffic. Most of the remaining 20 Class 342s active in Slovenia are now in the latest red livery and handle the majority of loco hauled passenger trains between Maribor and Ljubljana and also on other routes.

Class 362

Forty of these Bo-Bo-Bo articulated electric locomotives were built by ASGEN in Italy from 1960. Seventeen of the locos were taken into stock with the Slovenian Railways after the split up of the country. The class were designed for heavier passenger and freight trains especially on the steeply graded lines to Koper and Rijeka. Nos. 362.023, 362.026 and 362.027 were fitted with safety equipment for running into Italy in December 2001. In late 2008, Nos. 362.029 and 362.031 were sold to a private operator in the Czech Republic. Only a few now remain in use in Slovenia.

Class 363

Forty large Co-Co electric locomotives were built by Alsthom in France from 1975. Although the order actually consisted of 40 locomotives the final loco No. 363-040 was delivered as spare parts. In 1976 the original No. 363-002 was destroyed in a major accident when the loco ran into the rear of a loaded fuel train. No. 363-039 was renumbered as 363-002 on 1 October 1983 to take its place in the number sequence. The second No. 363-002 was then also involved in a severe accident on 18 August 2001 but luckily as the frame was not damaged the loco was repaired and returned to use.

In the days of JŽ operating the locos they used to work to Rijeka and also to the Port via the branch from Skrljevo - Bakar, but nowadays they only work to the border station at apjane. The steeply graded Koper line with its vast amount of freight traffic has always been a very busy route for the large Class 363, many trains having two or even three locos working the train to climb the hill. The locos can still sometimes be found on passenger trains and the daily fast train from Maribor to Koper is generally a Class 363 duty.

Class 541

In 2006 the first of the Krauss Maffei built *Taurus* locos entered traffic and with their dual voltage capabilities they soon took over working all the international passenger services between Jesenice and Dobova, replacing the need for a loco change at Jesenice. The class are split into two types; the Class 541.0 which are capable of working into Germany, Austria and Croatia and Class 541.1 which can also ⇨

Above: *Class 363 No. 363.004 passes Kranj with the summer dated Motorail train No. 1195 from Hamburg to Rijeka on 16 July 2005. This heavy train was exclusively hauled by a Class 363 loco within Slovenia. Note the one bi-level motorail wagon coupled directly behind the locomotive.* **Philip Wormald**

Left: *Class 664 No. 664.103 is viewed at Rakitovec on 25 April 2009 working the international train running for the summer season in 2009 from Hrpelje-Kozina to Pula. This train had been diesel multiple unit operated in the past few years so the return to loco hauled operation is a big bonus.* **Philip Wormald**

work into Italy and Croatia. The initial order of 20 locos were supplemented by a further order of 12 introduced from mid-2009. This final batch was ordered so that electric traction is available when the route from Pragersko - Murska Sobota - Hodoš is electrified in the next couple of years.

Class 642
These small French designed Bo-Bo locos are used for shunting duties throughout Slovenia. The class was introduced from 1961 and was the standard small shunting loco and also used on some branch line services. Seventeen locos were in service on Sž in 2008 and based at Divača, Ljubljana and Maribor. The locos can be found all over the system, especially shunting in the large yards at Ljubljana Zalog and also at Pragersko. No. 642.200 is now fitted with an Isotta Fraschini engine.

Class 643
A slightly later development of the class 642, 22 locos were in use in 2008, based at Ljubljana and Maribor. As with the Class 642 the locos are used on shunting duties throughout the network. Nos. 643.026, 643.028 and 643.043 are now fitted with Värtsilä engines and Nos. 643.032 and 643.040 are fitted with Isotta Fraschini engines.

Class 644
Twenty five General Motors type G12 were built by Macosa in Spain in 1974. The locos are fitted with a GM 12-645E engine and when delivered were fitted with train heating

boilers for use on passenger trains. The locos were designed for use on secondary lines and have a A1A-A1A wheel arrangement. All locos remained with Sž after the split from JŽ although a number were out of use for many years.

From 2004 a few locos were sold to Serbia for use on both freight and passenger trains, these locos were overhauled at Maribor before shipment. The remaining locos in Slovenia see use on freights on the line to Kočevje and Novo Mesto as well as sometimes helping out at Celje, Maribor and Nova Gorica as required. One loco can sometimes to found working the Avtovlak car carrying train between Bohinjska Bistrica and Most na Soci.

By mid-2009 Nos. 644.001, 644.002, 644.006, 644.009, 644.010 and 644.017 had been sold to Serbia and No. 644.003 (renumbered to 644.024), 644.007, 644.013 and 644.015 have been sold to Montenegro (Črna Gora). Meanwhile, Nos. 644.011 and 644.024 were cut up in late 2008 and the future of 644.020 does not look too hopeful at the time of writing.

Class 661
This class are the standard General Motors built G16 export model which was introduced from 1961. The locos have a Co-Co wheel arrangement and are fitted with a 16-567C engine rated at 1,900 hp. There was once a large fleet of locos in the days of the former Yugoslavia, but only five remained in Slovenia after the split up of the railways. Two of these were from the last 661.4 sub-series which had a low nose and were never fitted with any

form of train heating. Currently only Nos. 661.032 and 661.164 remain in use and almost always on freight duty assisting on Class 644 diagrams. The other three locos are stored at the works in Maribor.

Class 664
Twenty Class 664 Co-Co diesels were built locally by Đuro Đaković in Slavonski Brod under license from General Motors and were all allocated to the Slovenian area and remained there after the split.

The locos are Co-Co and have a 16-645E roots blown engine rated at 2,000 hp. The locos are fitted with electric train heating and are the only diesels in Slovenia with this capability.

The allocation is split between Maribor and Nova Gorica as well as one loco (normally 664.103) which is based at Divača for handling freight traffic on the Pula line. The locos at Maribor handle freight and passenger traffic on the line towards Hodoš and Čakovec and ⇨

Above: *Built locally in Solvenia by Đuro Đaković in Slavonski Brod under license from General Motors, Class 664 No. 664.117 is captured shortly after leaving Ormož with local train No. 3819 to Maribor on 22 April 2009. This train is normally operated by a two car diesel multiple unit, but due to a shortage of serviceable units, a two-car loco-hauled formation substituted on this date. Sadly it appears that at least the leading coach had been the subject of a vandal attack with graffiti on the lower body panels.* **Philip Wormald**

also freights on the line towards Bleiburg. One Maribor allocated loco is usually based at Celje for working freights to Rogatec and Velenje.

The locos at Nova Gorica work the freights between there and Jesenice, Ajdovščina and Sežana and can also sometimes assist on passenger trains during a shortage of serviceable DMUs.

Class 732

Three Class 732 diesel-hydraulic shunting locos are in service in Sž. They were built in 1970 by Đuro Đaković under licence from Jenbacher in Austria. The locos are all based in the Ljubljana division.

The multiple units

The Italian built 'Pendolino' electric multiple unit trains were introduced from 2000. The three sets are used exclusively on fast ICS (Inter City Slovenia) trains between Ljubljana and Maribor. A summer dated train sees a set continue through to Koper. Until early 2009 a set was used through to Venezia but due to lack of new required Italian signalling equipment this service has now ceased.

The multiple unit fleet for local trains is a mix of Italian and German built types and a number of lines are exclusively worked by these types. The EMU fleet is a mix of 30 Siemens Desiro units which were introduced from 2000. Ten are two-car sets and 20 are three-car sets. There are also six of the old Polish built Class 311s in use mainly on peak rush hour trains.

The DMU fleet consists of the German built Class 711 units built from 1970 for long distances service and were first class only configuration, six sets remain in use. The class 713s were built from 1984 and are fitted with a buckeye coupling, 25 sets are in use. Finally

the Class 813.0 are as built Fiat units with eight sets in use, and the 813.1 are sets that have been rebuilt by TVT in Slovenia, 31 are in use.

The Routes
(in Sž table order)

Table 10: Ljubljana - Dobova
The route heading east towards Croatia and the remainder of former Yugoslavia. This very attractive mainline closely follows the River Sava. All the international passenger trains are now worked by Class 541 or Austrian Class 1216 locos.

Table 20: Ljubljana - Jesenice
The attractive 64 kilometre route runs via Kranj and Lesce-Bled to Jesenice which is the border station with Austria. All international trains are now worked by Class 541 or 1216 'Taurus' locos and local trains with Desiro EMUs.

Table 21: Ljubljana - Kamnik Graben
This is a 25 km branch line running north from Ljubljana. All trains are DMU operated and a roughly hourly service throughout the day operates, but no service at weekends.

Table 30: Zidani Most - Maribor - entilj
Covers the route north towards Austria via Lako, Celje and Pragersko. This is another beautiful journey following the river as far as Celje. Classic curvy double track main line used by the few international trains from Austria. Pragersko is the junction station for trains to Croatia and Hungary.

Table 31: Celje - Velenje
A secondary DMU only line running North West from Celje with a length of 38 km. There

is quite a quite good weekday service but very limited Saturday service. Freight traffic consists of electrical goods being shipped from Velenje.

Table 32/33: Celje - Imeno / Sveti Rok ob Sotli
Another DMU branch, splitting at Stranje to serve Imeno and Rogatec / Sveti Rok ob Sotli. Both routes are former through lines to Croatia but now out of use over the border. The passenger service runs Mondays - Fridays and also a limited service on Sundays. There is freight traffic from Rogatec formed of glass which is produced in the factory close to the station.

Table 34: Maribor - Prevalje
A secondary DMU only line which follows the River Drava via Dravograd and to Bleiburg in Austria via Prevalje, services are operated by DMUs. A freight runs through to Austria via Bleiburg three days a week.

Table 40: Maribor - Ormoz - Središče
A local DMU service runs via Pragersko (a few trains run via the avoiding curve) via Ptuj and Ormoz. Two local trains a day continue to Cakovec in Croatia. Ptuj is the oldest town in Slovenia and is well worth a visit. The line can be quite busy with freight action between Pragersko and Ormoz as all trains must traverse this section.

Table 41: Ormoz - Murska Sobota - Hodo
The section north of Murska Sobota was opened on 16 May 2001 and has a few early morning trains and one through train a day in each direction to Budapest. A reasonable service operates between Ormoz and Murska Sobota. A few trains are hauled by the very popular and loud Class 664 diesels, but time ⇨

Above: *Class 664 No. 644.004 is viewed approaching □ikole on the morning of 22 April 2009, powering train No. 44770 running from Pragersko to the Croatian town of Čakovec, situated a short distance over the Slovenian border. The 2,000 installed horsepower of the General Motors prime mover needing all its strength to shift this load of 17 top-loading bogie hopper cars.* **Philip Wormald**

is running out as electrification is planned. The freight only line to Gorna Radgona branches off at Ljutomer and runs a few days a week and consists of the mineral water from the sources near Radenci.

Table 50: Ljubljana - Sežana
This is the main line for trains heading west of Ljubljana to Italy, also to Koper and to Rijeka, so is a busy route. Nowadays only one through train a day operates to Italy and this is an overnight train! The line is naturally very busy for freight traffic to and from Koper. A classic horse shoe curve exists at Borovnica which

allows the trains to start the climb as the head towards Divača and Sežana.

Table 61: Divača - Koper / Pula
As mentioned above the Koper line is very busy with freight traffic. In direct comparison to the line to Pula which sees very little traffic. There is usually one freight train a day and a through train direct to Pula only in the summer months. The Koper line is stunning and must rate as one of the all time great lines of Europe.

Table 64: Pivka - Ilirska Bistrica
The route to Rijeka which sees two through loco

hauled trains a day, one conveying a though couchette from München in the summer and the second through coaches from Wien. There are also two local trains over the border on weekdays.

Table 70: Jesenice - Nova Gorica - Sežana
The very beautiful 'Tranzalpine' route runs from the Austrian border south to within inches of the Italian border at Nova Gorica. All passenger trains operate with Fiat DMUs, but during shortage of these units Class 664s can sometimes deputise on loco-hauled stock or can pilot ailing units. One weekday freight runs each day on ⇨

Slovenia Fact File

National name:	Republic of Slovenia
Size:	20,151 sq km
Population:	2,053,740 (September 2008)
Capital:	Ljubljana
Main physical features:	A short coastal strip on the Adriatic, an alpine mountain region adjacent to Italy and Austria, mixed mountains and valleys with numerous rivers to the east
Climate:	Mediterranean climate on the coast, continental climate with mild to hot summers and cold winters in the plateaus and valleys to the east
Land Borders:	Austria 330 km, Croatia 670 km, Italy 232 km, Hungary 102 km
Visa requirements:	None for European residents
Time difference:	GMT +1hour
Major holidays:	1, 2 Jan, 8 Feb, Easter Monday, 27 Apr, 1, 2 May, Pentecost, 25 Jun, 15 Aug, 17 Aug, 15 Sep, 31 Oct, 1 & 23 Nov, 25, 26 Dec
Accommodation:	Numerous hotels and Motels
Reaching Slovenia:	Numerous flights from Europe and UK
Gauge:	1435 mm, (4ft 8.5 in)
Currency:	Euro
Tickets:	Inter Rail one country pass or local tickets
Reservations:	Only required on ICS Pendolino
Photography:	No restrictions
Security:	Generally very safe and relaxed
Health/food/general:	Excellent, very clean and good food

Web sites to check out:

Slovenske Zeleznice	http://www.slo-zeleznice.si/
Vlaki Railfan site	http://www.vlaki.net/

Below: *One of the three Pendolino sets in use on the Slovenian Railways is seen at Pragersko on 22 April 2009 forming train No. ICS12 (Inter City Slovenia) which runs from Ljubljana to Maribor. The three sets are almost exclusively used on Ljubljana - Maribor services, and on one summer dated train to Koper.* **Philip Wormald**

the north end of the line. South of Nova Gorica the line is busier as there are also freights entering Slovenia via the Gorizia - Nova Gorica border crossing. The famous 'Avtovlak' car train runs on the Bohinjska Bistrica - Most na Soci section and is worked by either a Class 644 or 664, one carriage and some car carrying vehicles.

Table 72: Nova Gorica - Ajdovščina
This 26 km branch line only has a service during the school term time. There is also a weekday freight usually powered by a Class 664.

Table 80: Ljubljana - Novo Mesto - Metlika
This line sees a regular DMU service on weekdays and a very basic service at weekends. There are limited connections over the border to Karlovac in Croatia, again with DMUs. Class 644s handle freight traffic in the Novo Mesto area and also on the freight only line from Grosuplje to Kocevje. The Renault car factory at Novo Mesto has cut down most of the freight that used to go by rail and now there is only general cargo and some timber traffic.

Table 82: Sevnica - Trebnje
This short 31km secondary line is served by a few trains on weekdays and by one pair of trains on a Sunday, no service on Saturdays. All trains are DMU operated.

How to get there?
Travelling from the UK direct flights operate to Ljubljana with easyJet and Adria airways. A good alternative (and often cheaper) is to use Ryanair to neighbouring Italy or Austria with a choice of Graz, Klagenfurt or Trieste airports all within close range of Slovenia.

Travelling by land would involve changing trains in Bruxelles or Paris, then via München and Salzburg. A journey time of just over 15 hours via Paris is very impressive! ∎

Below: The Class 363 fleet were built by Alstom in France from 1975. Some 30 years after being built, No. 363.001 grinds up the steep hill from Koper with a heavily loaded iron ore train on 14 July 2005. The train is being banked by sister loco No. 363.013. This loco would be uncoupled from the train at Hrpelje-Kozina and then continues to push (uncoupled) as far as Rodik from where it returns for its next assignment light engine.
Philip Wormald

Above: *Class 362 No. 362.031 approaches Litija on 18 July 2005 on an 'Optima' car carrying train. These trains operate each summer between Villach (Austria) and Kapikule (Turkey) and provide a comfy service for Turkish people living in Germany to return to their homeland.*
Philip Wormald

Below: *Class 342 No. 342.030 passes Litija powering a freight bound for Ljubljana on 18 July 2005. These relatively small locos can still see operation on some quite heavy freight duties. The Class 342s were built by ASGEN in Italy from 1968 for the then Yugoslavian Railways.*
Philip Wormald

Above: *One of the two-car Desiro EMUs is seen arriving at Litija on a local train bound for Ljubljana on 18 July 2005. The railway operates both two and three car versions of these Siemens built sets. The Desiro family of diesel and electric multiple unit trains are now to be found operating in a huge number of countries and as far afield as North America.*
Philip Wormald

Below: *Siemens (Krauss Maffei) built 'Taurus' electric loco of Class 541 No. 541.105 is seen passing through Borovnica on 24 April 2009 with an iron ore train from the Port of Koper and heading towards its destination in Austria. Two sub-classes of 'Taurus' introduced from 2006 operate in Solvenia 541.0 capable of working into Germany, Austria and Croatia and Class 541.1 which can also work into Italy.* Philip Wormald

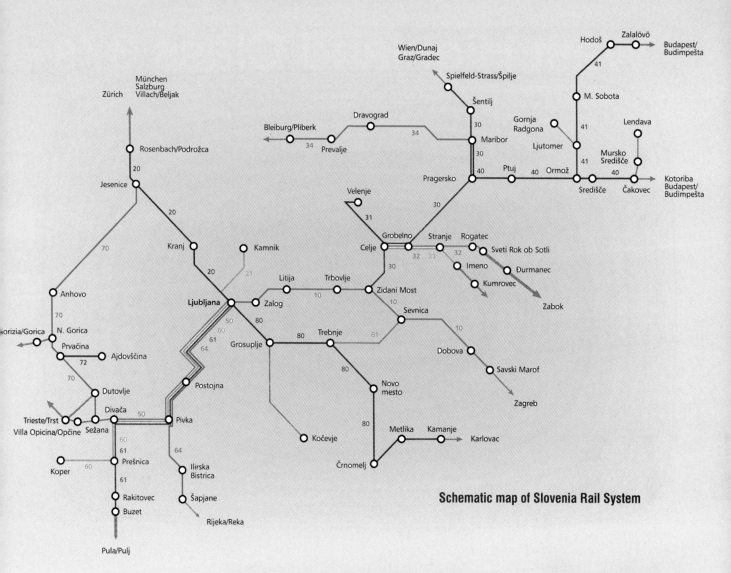

München
Salzburg
Zürich   Villach/Beljak

Wien/Dunaj
Graz/Gradec

Spielfeld-Strass/Špilje

Hodoš   Zalalövö   Budapest/
                          Budimpešta
41

Rosenbach/Podrožca   Šentilj   M. Sobota
20
Jesenice   30   41
                          Dravograd   Gornja   Lendava
20   Bleiburg/Pliberk   Radgona
                          34   Maribor   Ljutomer   Mursko
Kranj   Kamnik   34   Prevalje   30   41   Središče
                                    30   41
70   20   Velenje   40   Ptuj   40   Ormož   40   Kotoriba
                             31   Pragersko   Središče   Čakovec   Budapest/
Anhovo   21   30   Budimpešta
              Litija   Trbovlje   Grobelno   Stranje   Rogatec
70   Ljubljana   Zalog   Celje   32   33   32   Sveti Rok ob Sotli
N. Gorica   50   30   Imeno
Prvačina   60   10   Zidani Most   Kumrovec   Đurmanec
Gorizia/Gorica   61   80   10   Zabok
                 64   Grosuplje   80   Trebnje   81   Sevnica
Ajdovščina   Dobova
72   Savski Marof
70   Postojna   80   Novo   10
Dutovlje   mesto   Zagreb
Divača   50   Pivka   80
Trieste/Trst   64   Metlika   Kamanje   Karlovac
Villa Opicina/Opčine   Sežana   60   Kočevje   80
60   61   Ilirska   Črnomelj
Prešnica   Bistrica
Koper   60   61
61   Rakitovec   Šapjane

Buzet   Rijeka/Reka

Pula/Pulj

Schematic map of Slovenia Rail System

Right: *Class 664 No. 664.102 arrives at Murska Sobota station with train No. IC246 'Citadela' from Budapest Deli to Ljubljana on 22 April 2009. The train is diesel powered by a Class 664 between Hodo□and Pragersko.* **Philip Wormald**

West Highland Class 37s

By Chris Perkins

With the introduction of the English Electric Type 3, later to become Class 37, from the end of 1960, it was still to be a wait of several years before the class appeared on the West Highland route.

In 1968 Eastfield Depot received an allocation of five locomotives for use between Glasgow and Fort William on both passenger and freight workings. But their stay was short lived, as the Civil Engineers Department curtailed their use over the route. However, from the start of the summer 1981 timetable the class returned to take over most of the West Highland line duties, by which time Eastfield Depot had an allocation of 25 locomotives.

Because at this time the Class 37s were only fitted with steam train heating, the introduction of MkIII sleepers in 1983 brought about the need for the ETHELs that were converted from Class 25 locomotives to act as electric supply units. The first use of a Class 37 and an ETHEL was on the sleeper service on 3 October 1983 between Glasgow Queen Street and Fort William.

In 1985 the ETH fitted Class 37/4s were introduced and from then on were almost exclusively used as traction over the West Highland lines. This situation continued until 1989 when all services apart from the sleepers and freights went over to Class 156 DMU operation. The use of 37/4s continued on the sleeper services until 2006 when Class 67s took over.

Because of their light axle loadings the Class 37 is still the loco no operator can be without, so their appearance on charter trains, railtours and even the odd ballast working over the West Highland lines seems to be assured for the near future.

The following illustrations show the varied liveries carried by the class over the years. ∎

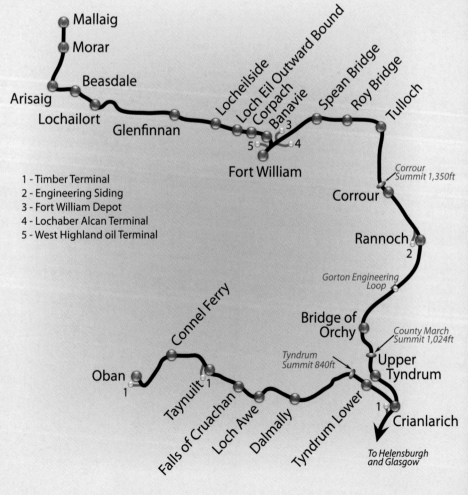

1 - Timber Terminal
2 - Engineering Siding
3 - Fort William Depot
4 - Lochaber Alcan Terminal
5 - West Highland oil Terminal

Above: *Looking most out of place on Rannoch Moor on 4 September 2000 is European Passenger Services operated No. 37604 as it approaches the remote Rannoch station powering train 7D54, the 11.58 Fort William to Coatbridge aluminium ingot service.* **Martin Loader**

Left Above: *ETH fitted Class 37/4 No. 37403* Isle of Mull *pilots failed Class 37/0 No. 37261* Caithness *and the southbound 'Royal Scotsman' as it breasts the summit at County March near Tyndrum on 20 May 1987. No. 37261 had failed earlier and No. 37403 had been removed from the 12.23 Mossend to Corpach freight at Bridge of Orchy to rescue the prestigious train.* **John Whiteley**

Below: *'Royal Scotsman' maroon-liveried No. 37416 passes Corpach with the Corpach Paper Mill to Fort William Yard trip working on 22 April 2005. The ECC bogie tank wagons will later be attached to the rear of the Fort William to Mossend Alcan service.* **Phil Wright**

THE WEST HIGHLANDER

London-Oban (for Iona)-Fort William-
Mallaig-Edinburgh-London

INTERCITY

Above: *Painted in large logo livery, No. 37402 Oor Wullie heads over County March summit on 20 May 1987 powering the 15.22 Mallaig Junction to Mossend. Air brake freight formed of just 10 four-wheel wagons. The peak of Ben Dorian dominates the background.*
John Whiteley

1995 ✳ Class 37 powered freights through Crianlarich ✳ 2000

1995

Time	Headcode	Train	Type of train	Traction
12.50 SX	7Y45	09.45 Coatbridge - Fort William	Empty Flats	Transrail 37
13.00 SX	7D19	10.35 Fort William - Coatbridge	Aluminium Ingots	2x Transrail 37s
01.15 MX	6S54	15.30 Blyth - Fort William	Loaded Alumina Tanks	2x Transrail 37s
02.15 SX	6E16	23.20 Fort William - Blyth	Empty Alumina Tanks	2x Transrail 37s

2000

Time	Headcode	Train	Type of train	Traction
07.25 SX	6Y42	05.00 Mossend - Oban/Taynuilt	Empty Timber OTAs	EWS 37
08.50 SO	7Y07	05.58 Coatbridge - Fort William	Empty Flats	EWS 37
09.00 SX	6Y45	06.36 Mossend - Fort William	Enterprise	EWS 37
11.35 TThO	7Y15	08.43 Coatbridge - Fort William	Empty Flats	EWS 37
13.15 SX	6D55	11.42 Oban - Mossend	Enterprise, Timber	EWS 37
15.15 MWFO	7D54	11.58 Fort William - Coatbridge	Aluminium Ingots	EWS 37
17.30 SX	7D60	15.00 Fort William - Mossend	Enterprise	2 x EWS 37s
20.15 SX	6E16	17.11 Fort William - Blyth	Empty Alumina tanks	EWS 37
21.35 SX	6S54	08.50 Blyth - Fort William	Loaded Alumina tanks	2 X EWS 37s

Information supplied by Freightmaster Ltd

Above Left: *Painted in Royal Scotsman livery, No. 37416 heads a Scottish Railway Preservation Society railtour from Mallaig to Linlithgow over Loch Nan Umah viaduct on the Mallaig extension. On 11 June 2005. Sister loco No. 37417 was on the rear of the train.*
Phil Wright

Right: *Very much the old order of the West Highland, with semaphore signals and rail blue liveried locos. Here, rail blue, split headcode box Class 37/0 No. 37037 double heads Class 27 No. 27038 south from Crianlarich with the 08.00 Oban to Glasgow Queen Street on 13 May 1985.* Jim Binnie

Coaster & Sprinter Network

To Los Angeles

- Oceanside
  - Coast Highway
    - Crouch Street
      - El Camino Real
        - Rancho Del Ore
          - College Blvd
            - Melrose Drive
- Carlsbad Village
  - Vista Transit Center
- Carlsbad Poinsettia
  - Escondido Ave
  - Buena Creek
- Encinitas
  - Palomar College
  - San Marcos Civic Center
  - Cal State San Marcos
- Solana Beach
  - Nordahl Road
  - Escondido
- Sorrento Valley
- Old Town San Diego
- San Diego

To Tijuana (Mexico)

Pacific Ocean

Coaster Service
Sprinter Service

N

Above: *In March 2008 the 22 mile Oceanside to Escondido line opened to passengers using a fleet of 12 Siemens-built, Mercedes diesel-powered two-car units. The trains usually operated in pairs and work a half-hourly service over the route all day. Set No. 4008 departs from Coast Highway bound for Oceanside on 6 October 2008. CJM*

Below: *Running unprotected from the Coast Highway and surrounding streets, a southbound Coaster train, led by Cab Car No. 2310 traverses the double track section at San Eljio near control point Cardiff on 6 October 2008 forming train No. 656, the 15.35 Oceanside to San Diego. In usual operation the locomotives are worked on the north end of trains. CJM*

Far Left: *Powered by Motive Power Industries rebuilt F40PH 3C No. SDNR 2105, the 09.45 San Diego to Oceanside (train 639) traverses the single line section past the spectacular beach at Del Mar on 8 October 2008. CJM*

Left: *The evening commute heads north from San Diego on the evening of 6 October 2008. Photographed departing from Solana Beach station, the 15.40 San Diego to Oceanside powered by SDNR 2103 leads its formation of five double-deck passenger cars towards control point Craven and entry to the single line section to control point Cardiff. CJM*

Los Angeles Metrolink Network

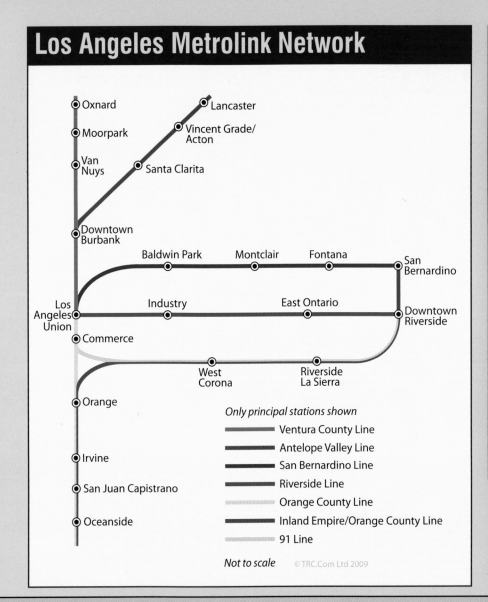

Oxnard
Lancaster
Moorpark
Vincent Grade/ Acton
Van Nuys
Santa Clarita
Downtown Burbank
Baldwin Park
Montclair
Fontana
San Bernardino
Los Angeles Union
Industry
East Ontario
Downtown Riverside
Commerce
West Corona
Riverside La Sierra
Orange
Irvine
San Juan Capistrano
Oceanside

Only principal stations shown

Ventura County Line
Antelope Valley Line
San Bernardino Line
Riverside Line
Orange County Line
Inland Empire/Orange County Line
91 Line

Not to scale   © TRC.Com Ltd 2009

Below: *With a five-car formation behind, F59PH No. 860 slows for the Downtown Burbank stop on 1 October 2008 forming train 215 the 17.00 Los Angeles Union to Lancaster. The Metrolink network is very well used in the morning and evening commute, with all stations having free car parking in an attempt to reduce the automobile traffic in downtown LA.* **CJM**

Above: *The main hub of Metrolink activity is Los Angeles Union station, opened in 1939 with the cooperation of the Union Pacific and Atchison Topeka & Sante Fe Railroads. Today it is used by Metrolink, Amtrak and MetroRail. In this 15 May 2009 view, two Metrolink trains occupy the platforms with empty stock for the car sheds after arriving with morning commuter services. The train nearest the camera is led by No. 898, one of the latest fleet of 13 Motive Power Industries-built MP36PH-3C units, on the left is F59PH No. 857. CJM*

Below: *Led by one of the 2001 built FP59PHI fleet No. 884, train No. 850, the 07.30 Oceanside to Riverside passes over the BNSF/UP West Riverside Junction on 9 October 2008 with a four vehicle formation. Metrolink trains are usually formed that locomotives lead away from Los Angeles Union station. CJM*

Above: The main Metrolink bi-level passenger stock was built by Bombardier Transportation between 1992-2002 with a mix of 'coach' and 'cab-cars', sadly a number of vehicles have been written off since the passenger service was inaugurated and some hire-in of vehicles from other administrations has taken place. One of the 1992-93 built cab cars No. 616, of the design with one front window and a door window, departs from Glendale on 23 March 2008 forming the 08.35 Burbank Airport to Los Angeles Union service. CJM

Below: The Metrolink location of Chatsworth on the Ventura Line hit world news on 12 September 2008 when train 111, the 15.35 Los Angeles union to Moorpark collided head on with a Union Pacific freight, sadly the engineer and 24 passenger lost their lives. This view shows train 111 approaching the Chatsworth stop on 1 October 2008 with 1997 built cab car No. 636 (one of the vehicles with two end windows) bringing up the rear. On the front of the three-car formation is FP59PHI No. 879. CJM

Metrolink Loco Factfile

Number Range	Type	Notes
800	F40PH	Ex Amtrak 396
851-873	F59PH	
874-873	F59PHI	
884-887	F59PHI	
888-902	MP36PH-3C	

Reporting mark - SCRA

F40PH = General Motors built, 3000hp
F59PH = General Motors built, 3000hp
F59PHI = General Motors built, 3000hp
MP36PH-3C = Motive Power Inc, 3600hp

Above: *The line to Oceanside gets an infrequent Metrolink service from either San Bernardino or Los Angeles union. Powered by F59PH No. 853, the 13.10 from Downtown Riverside passes the infrequently used San Clemente Pier station on 8 October 2008 bound for Riverside. The 'X2' sign on the right indicates that the engineer of a northbound train should sound his horn for two passenger crossings ahead.* CJM

Left: *The original Santa Fe station at San Bernardino now houses the five platform station facility used by Metrolink. On 8 September 2005, cab car 628 departs forming the 14.00 to Los Angeles union. On the left is the huge BNSF intermodal terminal and container sidings. The bridge which crosses the station provides an excellent vantage point from which to observe and photograph trains.* CJM

Right: *In 2008 a small batch of new locos were delivered to Metrolink from builder Motive Power Industries in Boise, Idaho. These entered traffic in 2009 along with new passenger stock and cab cars. Reflecting the original order of the day, General Motors (EMD) F59PH No. 861 leads a four car formation passing Prado Dam near West Corona forming train 704, the 12.45 Los Angeles Union to Riverside.* CJM

Surfliner Network

To San Jose/Oakland and Northern Caliornia

- ● San Luis Obispo
- ● Grover Beach
- ● Guadalupe / Santa Maria
- ● Lampoc Surf
- ● Goleta
- ● Santa Barbara
- ● Carpinteria
- ● Ventura
- ● Oxnard
- ● Camarillo
- ● Moorpark
- ● Semi Valley
- ● Chatsworth
- ● Van Nuys
- ● Burbank Airport
- ● Glendale
- ● Los Angeles Union
- ● Fullerton
- ● Anaheim
- ● Santa Ana
- ● Irvine
- ● San Juan Capistrano
- ● San Clemente Pier
- ● Oceanside
- ● Solana Beach
- ● San Diego

© TRC.Com Ltd 2009

Above: *The main Amtrak network operates over the principal routes in California, with five named services. Traversing Northern California's 'Sea Wall' near Hercules, P32s Nos. AMK118 and AMK119 power train No. 11, the 10.00 Seattle (of 8 May) to Los Angeles Union 'Coast Starlight. This train from Seattle to Los Angeles is a notorious late runner, frequently recorded between four and six hours late, on the day this picture was taken, 9 May 2007, it was a mere three and a half hours behind schedule. CJM*

Amtrak Network for California Routes

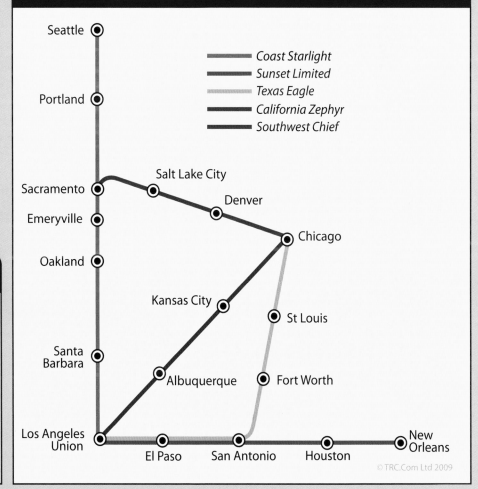

Coast Starlight
Sunset Limited
Texas Eagle
California Zephyr
Southwest Chief

Seattle

Portland

Salt Lake City
Sacramento
Denver
Emeryville
Chicago

Oakland

Kansas City
St Louis

Santa
Barbara
Albuquerque
Fort Worth

Los Angeles
Union
New
Orleans
El Paso   San Antonio   Houston

© TRC.Com Ltd 2009

Amtrak Loco Factfile
(Mainline diesel)

Number Range	Type	Notes
1-207	P42DC	
464-470	FP59PHI	
500-519	P32-8	
700-717	P32-ACDM	
800-843	P42DC	Rebuilt from P40
90200-90368	NPCU	Cab cars x F40PH

Reporting mark - AMTK

P42 = General Electric built, 4200hp
F59PHI = General Motors built, 3000hp
P32-8 = General Electric built, 3200hp
P32-ACDM = 4000hp

Above: *Amtrak California operate the Capitol and San Joaquin routes, and in so doing traverse the streets of Oakland as they approach the Jack London Square stop from Emeryville. FP59PHI No. 2013 runs parallel with a Union Pacific freight led by SD70 No. 4394 on 7 April 2008. Photography of the street running section is easy and usually generates little problems. For UK rail enthusiasts it is quite amazing how trains, road vehicles and pedestrians share the highway - normally without any confliction. CJM*

Left: *On occasions if members of the Amtrak California fleet are not available, locos from the core Amtrak fleet are rostered. On 6 March 2006, Dash8-P32 No. 505 was called into service and is captured in non-typical Californian rain as it awaits departure from Bakersfield with the 13.15 service to Oakland. The station at Bakersfield provides a very modern integrated bus and rail hub. CJM*

Amtrak California - Capitol Corridor & The San Joaquins Routes

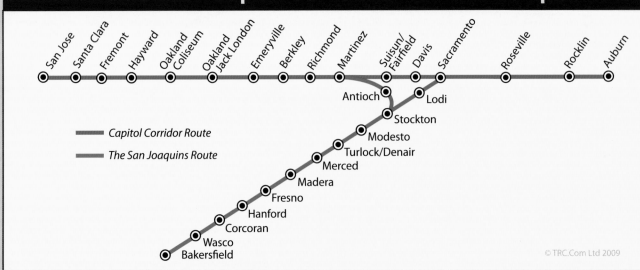

San Jose · Santa Clara · Fremont · Hayward · Oakland Coliseum · Oakland Jack London · Emeryville · Berkley · Richmond · Martinez · Suisun/Fairfield · Davis · Sacramento · Roseville · Rocklin · Auburn

Antioch

Lodi

Stockton

Modesto

Turlock/Denair

Merced

Madera

Fresno

Hanford

Corcoran

Wasco

Bakersfield

▬▬▬ Capitol Corridor Route

▬▬▬ The San Joaquins Route

© TRC.Com Ltd 2009

Caltrain Network

To Southern California
Los Angeles

- Tamien
- San Jose
- College Park
- Santa Clara
- Lawrence
- Sunnyvale
- San Antonio
- California Avenue
- Stanford
- Palo Alto
- Menlo Park
- Atherton
- Redwood City
- San Carlos
- Belmont
- Hillside
- Hayward Park
- San Mateo
- Burlingame
- Broadway
- Millbrae
- San Bruno
- South San Francisco
- Bayshore
- 22nd Street
- San Francisco

© TRC.Com Ltd 2009

Amtrak-California Loco Factfile

Number Range	Type	Notes
2001-2015	FP59PHI	General Motors built, 3200hp
2051-2052	P32-8	General Electric built, 3200hp
Reporting mark - CDTX		

Caltrain Loco Factfile

Number Range	Type	Notes
900-922	F40PH2	General Motors built, 3200hp
923-928	MP36PH-3C	MPI built, 3600hp
Reporting mark - JPBX		

Top: *The Caltrain service linking San Francisco with San Jose and Tamien is a busy network. Tailed by one of the modern MP36PH-3C locos No. 926, the 10.10 San Jose to San Francisco sets off on its journey on 13 October 2008.* **CJM**

Above: *Two types of cab-car are found on the Caltrain network, those of the original design (seen centre) and the more recently introduced 'Baby Bullet' sets seen on the outside. This view is recorded at San Jose station.* **CJM**

Below: *Locos usually operate on the south or San Jose end of Caltrain services, with a mix of P40PH2s and MP36PH-3Cs. This is the view of San Francisco station in the afternoon light.* **CJM**

Above: *Light rail is a major part of daily commuting life in the larger conurbations of California, with sizeable networks operating in San Diego, Los Angeles and San Francisco. The Trolley network in San Diego is a credit to any city in the world, with a three line intense network radiating from the City down as far south as the Mexico border. This is the view of the station at San Ysidro, the crossing point from the USA to Tijuana in Mexico. The trolley trains usually operate in six car formations at around five minute intervals and are frequently crowded. Trolleys 1005 and 1022 await departure to downtown San Diego on 7 October 2008. CJM*

Left Middle: *The City of Los Angeles is a very busy city and is supported by an intense public transport service which seems to operate most efficiently. The main Los Angeles Union station is served by the Metro Rail Gold line which provides a link to the City of Pasadena with a modernised segregated and street running route. Recently a number of new vehicles have been delivered to this line for expansion deeper into the downdown Los Angeles area. A twin formation is seen departing from Los Angeles Union while Amtrak P32 Nos. 83 and 115 arrive at Los Angeles Union, with train 21 the 'Texas Eagle' from Chicago on 10 October 2008. CJM*

Left Bottom: *The Los Angeles Metro Rail network, while centred on the downtown city area of Los Angeles, also serves Long Beach, with the blue line, opened in 1990 providing a 15min interval service from 06.00 to 23.00 daily. The trains usually of six car length are operated by Nippon-built stock and work in tunnel sections within the downtown area of Los Angeles, street running and segregated running. Led by vehicle 105 a six car formation arrives at the Transit Mall stop in Long Beach on 3 April 2008. The service from downtown Los Angeles to Long Beach takes around one hour, with very heavy passenger loadings. CJM*

Above: *The City of San Francisco has long been famed for its cable cars and street cars providing an amazing public transport and tourist attraction in the city. The San Francisco Muni-operated 'F' line from Castro to Fishermans Wharf is operated by historic street cars. These are mainly PCC vehicles refurbished from various cities across the US, but these are supplemented by some wonderfully restored truly vintage stock. One such car is No. 952 built originally in 1923 for use in New Orleans, Louisiana. Now restored to green and red livery the car is seen on an 'F' line service calling at Pier 39 bound for the Jones turnround. In the background the ocean liner* **Norwegian Sun** *can be seen docked in the ocean liner terminal at pier 33. CJM*

Right Middle: *In terms of photography, if you want to take pictures of the PCC or any of the 'F' line street cars no better place can be found than the turnround point at Jones, here in the morning anything up to five street cars can be found basking in the sun. This view shows three vehicles led by No. 1056 painted in the black and cream livery of Kansas City. CJM*

Right Bottom: *In addition to the historic street cars and cable cars, the City of San Francisco Muni network operates modern trams on longer distance lines radiating both north and south of the main city area. These two-vehicle articulated vehicles perform street running, segregated operation and tunnel operation and offer a good travelling environment at low cost. Set 1457 is seen near the Caltrain station on a 'T' line service to Sunndale and Bayshore. At this point the vehicle is operating on a segregated running section. CJM*

Oils to Westerleigh

By Chris Perkins

The Murco Oil Terminal is located in the Westerleigh Railhead, South Gloucestershire. It is situated at the end of a short single track branch that diverges from the Bristol to Birmingham main line at Yate. The branch is the truncated remains of the Midland Railway line to Bath and Bristol via Mangotsfield. The Railhead also contains the now out of use refuse transfer station for South Gloucestershire.

Westerleigh depot is the largest of Murco's terminals serving the South West and parts of South Wales. It was built in 1990 and was rail connected from the outset and receives 55 loaded 100-ton TEA bogie tank wagons six days a week in two block trains. One arrives in the early morning from the Lindsey refinery at Immingham and the other at lunchtime from Robeston in South Wales.

The Lindsey train is formed of 27 tanks while the Robeston train has 28 wagons, and due to the weight of these trains they require Class 60 haulage. On arrival the train splits into two sections for unloading, with the train engine carrying out the shunting. The locomotive then remains parked outside the terminal compound until required to reform the train for the return journey.

The train from Lindsey is due to arrive at 05.03 running as the 6V98 and departs at 11.41 as train 6E41, although some days it can depart as early as 10.30. In addition, some Wednesday workings can originate from the Port Clarence refinery and have been Class 66 hauled in recent times but these run to the same paths.

The Robeston train arrives at 12.20 as train 6B13 and is booked to depart at 17.42 as train 6B47. On Saturdays the times vary slightly with 6E41 departing at 10.13 and 6B47, which terminates at Margam Yard departs at 16.40. The same locomotive can stay on either diagram for several days.

It had been the wish of DBS to eradicate the Class 60 from its traction fleet by April 2009, but currently there is no other motive power in the fleet that can handle the current weight of these trains.

The only options available, which were not really feasible, was the running of trains as two portions, this causes major pathing problems for Network Rail and requires extra handling staff at the terminals to be available for longer periods. The other option is double heading, but this would mean the trains would be too long to fit into pathing loops over the route, and therefore Class 60s currently remain the booked power. In summer 2009 only 10 operational Class 60s out of the original fleet of 100 remain, so it will be interesting to see how DBS tackles this problem. ■

Above: *No. 60081* Isambard Kingdom Brunel *passes below Purton Manor on 15 August 2003, on the banks of the River Severn with train 6B13 from Robeston refinery to Westerleigh.* Chris Perkins

Previous Page: *Class 60 No. 60011 looks fairly clean with its patched paintwork as it exits Wickwar Tunnel powering 6B13 loaded tanks from Robeston to Westerleigh Murco Depot on 1 April 2009.* Chris Perkins

Left: *No. 60035 passes Kidney Hill on the approach to Westerleigh Railhead with the service from Robeston on 30 October 2007. This section of line has since been re-laid and some vegetation clearance has taken place, improving photographic viewpoints.* Chris Perkins

Below: *An overall view of the Murco Depot at Westerleigh Railhead showing the TEA wagons from train 6V98 split into two portions for unloading, while train locomotive No 60074* Teenage Spirit *waits outside the gates of the complex to reform the empties before departing as 6E41 on 5 March 2008.* Chris Perkins

Above: *Soon after starting its return journey to Lindsey oil refinery, celebrity '60' No. 60040* **The Territorial Army Centenary** *heads towards Wickwar Tunnel powering train 6E41, the empty tanks from Westerleigh on 28 May 2009. When released to traffic in 2008, this was one of the first two locos to carry the DB-Schenker bodyside branding, the other being powder blue-liveried No. 60074.* **Chris Perkins**

Below: *No 60091* **An Teallach** *has been routed over the 'up' fast line and is passing under the 'up' slow line at Bishton flyover on 9 February 2009 powering train 6B13 loaded TEA tanks from Robeston to Westerleigh.* **Chris Perkins**

North East Class 56 Action

By Chris Perkins

The Class 56 design was born in 1973 when British Rail needed a more powerful and dedicated freight locomotive for merry-go-round coal workings which were mainly in the hands of the underpowered Class 47s and pairs of Class 20s.

Brush Traction at Loughborough won the contract to build 135 locomotives but, due to space limitations at the works, the first 30 were built by Electroputere in Romania. The first example entered traffic in England on 27 February 1977 but, because of very poor build quality the Romanian built locomotives spent long periods out of service with reliability problems. Because of this British Rail decided to take over the production in it's own workshops. BREL Doncaster Works built 85 locomotives, but after this space was needed to take on the Class 58 project, and the final 20 locos were built at BREL Crewe Works.

The North East received a number of the class mainly for merry-go-round work but could also be seen powering oil, stone and metals trains. In October 1987 the FBYB Coal Sector at Blyth had 23 allocations including all the final Crewe-built locomotives.

Because of their very rushed design and build, the Class 56 fleet remained problematical all of their working career, and had a very low availability record often no better than 71 per cent, and most of the Romanian-built examples had been withdrawn by 1998.

Following the introduction of the EMD Class 66 by EWS, no less than 41 were withdrawn between January 1999 and March 2000, with the rest of the fleet following until the last two were withdrawn after railtour duties in April 2004. This resulted in a much shorter working life than would normally be the case. ∎

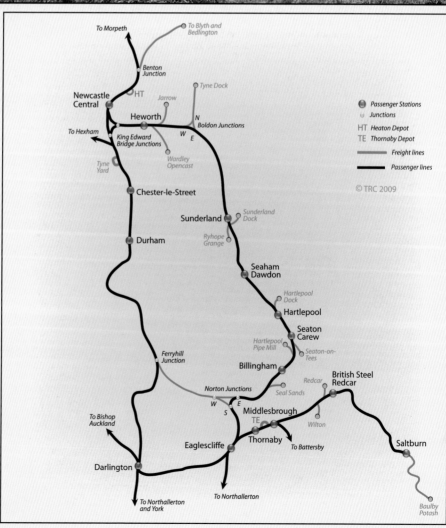

Above: *Crewe Works built No. 56119 crosses Freemans level crossing with the 15.24 North Blyth to Lynemouth loaded aluminia train on 11 September 2002. No 56119 remained operational until the end of fleet operations, being withdrawn in March 2004.* **Scott Borthwick**

Above left: *With the North Sea as a backdrop No. 56072 rounds the cliff top at Hunt Cliff with empties from Middlesbrough Goods to Boulby Mine on 5 May 2003. No 56072 almost made it to the end of class operations, being withdrawn in February 2004.* **John Whiteley**

Below: *No. 56113 a Doncaster Works built locomotive passes the signal box at Marchey's level crossing on the Blyth and Tyne route returning empty Alcan wagons to the loading point at North Blyth from Lynemouth on 11 June 2003. No 56113 was withdrawn in March 2004.* **Bob Lumley**

Above: *Stockton Cut Junction is where the line from Hartlepool joins the line from Thornaby and Middlesbrough to the east of Eaglescliffe.* *No 56046 painted in Dutch livery passes the junction with a Hartlepool to Immingham pipe train on 22 July 1996. No. 56046 was withdrawn from service in July 2006.* **Martin Loader**

Below: *No. 56127 in Trainload Freight coal sector livery and carrying out duties for which it was designed, passes Hendon near Sunderland with a loaded MGR on 4 September 1992. Although a late built Crewe loco, this member was withdrawn in February 2002.* **CJM**

Eurostar Barrier Flats

Number	Former Number	Note
6380	96380/86386	
6381	96381/86187	
6382	96382/86295	
6383	96383/86664	
6384	96384/86955	
6385	96385/86515	Modified to 6321
6386	96386/86859	Modified to 6322
6387	96387/86973	Modified to 6323
6388	96388/86562	Modified to 6324
6389	96389/86135	Modified to 6321

Right Top and Right Middle: *Numerically the final five of the original Eurostar barrier flats were sold to Siemens to act as barrier vehicles to their expanding fleet of Desiro EMU and DMU stock. The vehicles were overhauled by the LNWR works at Crewe and received a number of modifications for their new role. All are officially allocated to the Siemens depot in Northampton but can be found at any depot which deals with Desiro stock. For their Desiro use, one end of some vehicles was modified to have a fixed Dellner coupling while the other end retained the hinged coupling unit. The picture above right shows vehicle No. 6323 from its hinged coupling end, while the picture Right Middle shows the Desiro fixed coupling. Dual low level air brake and main reservoir pipes are fitted, while two connections are also provided to the hinged coupler providing automatic main reservoir and brake pipe connections. CJM*

Miscellaneous Barriers

Number	Former Number	Notes
975858	21033	BREL/Tanzanian stock barrier
975861	9239	BREL/Tanzanian stock barrier
977021	21098	BREL Crewe Works barrier
977022	21190	BREL Crewe Works barrier

Above: *A number of miscellaneous barrier and coupling adaptor vehicles have operated over the years to connect vehicles with different couplings together. These have been used for transporting export stock to docks and moving centre buffer vehicles around the network. However some of the most unusual adaptor vehicles were assembled for hauling the Southern Railway/BR-operated Waterloo & City stock over the main line. These units were fitted with London Underground type Ward couplers and a pair of four-wheel flat wagons were modified with Ward couplers at one end. The barriers are shown here flanking a Waterloo & City car at Wimbledon, powered by a Class 73 electro diesel. CJM*

First Generation DMMUs
Local service modernisation from the late 1950s

Above: *A classic view of a pair of Swindon Cross Country three-car sets, (later BR Class 120) are seen near Aynho Junction, south of Banbury on 29 August 1962. The six-car set is forming the 16.08 Birmingham Snow Hill to Paddington via Oxford. The leading vehicle is Driving Motor No. 50688, built at Swindon Works in 1957.* **Michael Mensing**

Despised by many enthusiasts when first introduced in the 1950s, the Diesel Mechanical Multiple Unit (DMMU) revolutionised the travel for millions of people throughout the UK and provided a service on many lines which might well have closed.

Like much of the early British Rail modernisation it lacked leadership and direction and thus we saw a vast number of different types of multiple unit train designed, built and introduced. This led to major resourcing problems with spare parts and an excessive training of depot and operations staff.

Today, views of the older diesel multiple unit classes are much sought after by enthusiasts, with the DMMU now having an almost cult following. The vast majority of preserved lines in the UK now sport at least one DMU on their roster, and these frequently provide an 'off-peak 'passenger service when it would be too expensive to operate steam or main line diesel power.

DMMU stock was built by no less than nine manufacturers - Birmingham RC&W, BR Derby, BR Swindon, Cravens, Gloucester RC&W, Metro Cammell, Park Royal, Pressed Steel and Wickham. Metro Cammell as a private builder and BR Derby were by far the largest suppliers.

With products emerging from these major works, external designs were obviously going to be different, some were more pleasing to the eye than others, with varying designs having either two or three front end windows, body or roof mounted destination indicators and either two or four character 'headcode' boxes.

Being multiple unit vehicle formations from one to four vehicles could operate as a 'set' with multiple coupling of up to three sets to form a train of up to 12 coaches.

All 'new' DMMU stock emerged in then BR green livery, but this was far from standard with differing shades recorded from most workshops.

The DMMU build was broken down into a number of internal design layouts, some

vehicles were designated as 'high-density' with exterior doors by each seating bay, these were used on busy mainly city orientated routes where high volumes of passengers were carried. Outer suburban units were built for the slightly longer distance routes with doors at vehicle ends and towards the centre, while a fleet of low density cross-country sets were built for the slower main line services over longer distances. These sets had a high quality interior finish and offered both first and second (third) class accommodation.

When originally introduced the requirement for a high visibility front end was not on the agenda and most sets carried a light yellow or cream 'whisker' banding on driving car ends. By the mid 1960s small yellow warning ends were progressively applied, frequently spoiling the pleasing body lines of the stock. The illustrations in this photo feature have been selected to show the diesel multiple unit scene in the late 1950s early 1960s period. ∎

Above: *A view which is hardly recognisable today, is this looking out of Glasgow Queen Street towards Cowlairs Tunnel. The amazing semaphore gantry has long since gone, and most of the daylight over the station has gone with the building of above station office blocks. This view of a Cross Country or InterCity DMU with a DMBC leading was recorded on 13 May 1961 and the photographer records it was the 10.00 from Edinburgh Waverley, a service which still operates today, but is now formed of a Class 170.* **Michael Mensing**

Right: *The introduction of DMU stock promoted the railway to operate low-cost specials for sporting events and frequently offered services to local events, such as this Stoke City v Huddersfield Town football match held in Stoke at the Victoria Ground on Boxing Day 1959. Even an outline drawing of a DMU was included and the train advertised as a 'Diesel Excursion'.* **CJM Collection**

Below: *Led by vehicle No. 56291, a four car formation stops at Acock's Green on 23 March 1961 forming the 16.05 Leamington Spa to Birmingham Moor Street service. The three-car set on the rear, built by Gloucester RC&W, sports all over green livery, while the driving trailer on the front has a waist height and cant rail height cream bodyside band.* **Michael Mensing**

Above: *Some of the physical cross country services were operated by general low-density units, such as this BR Derby built twin set pausing at Sandy in Bedfordshire on August Bank Holiday Monday 7 August 1961, forming the 14.12 Cambridge to Bletchley. At the time, this was part of the through route from Cambridge to Oxford, with a limited through service and others using either Bedford or Bletchley as a terminating point.* Michael Mensing

Right Above: *With a four-character route indicator on the front end, this three-car formation of Swindon Cross Country stock with Driving Motor Second No. 51586 nearest the camera, makes a shunt move through Worcester Shrub Hill station on 9 September 1961 and heads for the depot. It is interesting to note that only one marker light is located on the front end.* Michael Mensing

Right Below: *Devoid of cream front end whiskers, this four car local formation departing from Hampton-in-Arden on 13 September 1959 while forming the 14.35 Birmingham New Street to Coventry, is formed of a two-car Park Royal and two-car Metro Cammell set. The Park Royal set, led by a driving trailer composite (note the curtains in the seating bays behind the driving cab). These Park Royal sets, of which just 20 were built, were not the most successful of DMMUs and were phased out of service at an early date. The unit on the rear is a standard Metro-Cammel (later Class 101) twin set, operating in multiple with the Park Royal by means of the blue square multiple coupling equipment.* Michael Mensing

Above: *Derby Works-built 'lightweight' single Driving Motor Brake No. M79900 stands under what was left of the once overall roof at Banbury Merton Street station on 25 August 1960, while awaiting departure with the 13.55 to Buckingham. On this pleasant afternoon, the driver is seen sitting on the station seat with a cup of tea. Banbury Merton Street station opened in 1850 as the terminus of the Buckinghamshire Railway and closed to passengers on 2 January 1961.* **Michael Mensing**

Below: *Gloucester Railway Carriage & Wagon Works built a small fleet of two-car sets, later classified as Class 100. These rather attractive sets, with a shaped three window front end, destination blind above and two-character headcode on the front, were originally painted in all-over BR green with a cream band at waist and cant rail height. On 5 September 1959 a mixed GRC&W and Metro-Cammell four-car set led by vehicle No. 50354 arrives at Stechford forming the 12.50 Birmingham New Street to Coventry service.* **Michael Mensing**

Above: *The most numerous of the private-built DMMU vehicles emerged from the Birmingham factory of Metro-Cammell, who produced a distinctive cab end design which remained common on the rail network until the end of regular DMMU operation. In green livery with cream whisker end, a Metro-Cammell twin set led by a driving trailer departs from Alnmouth on Saturday 29 May 1962 forming the 14.10 Newcastle to Alnwick stopping service.* **Michael Mensing**

Below: *Towards the middle of the 1960s, the arbitrary yellow warning panel was applied to all leading DMMU vehicles, in an attempt to improve the sight line of an approaching train to track workers. With yellow panel applied, a three-car set of Derby-built high-density stock departs from Tyseley station on 2 September 1966, working as the 13.00 Leamington Spa to Birmingham Moor Street. At this time with no painted 'set' numbers and trains usually referred to by individual coach numbers, cab mounted unit formation and duty numbers were frequently applied in the non-driving front window, as in this case with the No. 302. In common with then standard practise, the British Railways lion and wheel roundel was only applied to the middle of powered vehicles.* **Michael Mensing**

Above: *Led by Driving Motor Brake No. 50423, a three car Birmingham RC&W set is viewed between north and middle Harecastle tunnels north of Stoke-on-Trent on 26 September 1960 while working the 13.15 Manchester Piccadilly to Birmingham New Street service. It appears that the train was well loaded with faces by each window position. Note the red triangular 'no smoking' signs in the side windows of the first two seating bays.* Michael Mensing

Right Above: *With distinct signs of where the front end cream whiskers have been replaced by a yellow warning panel, a pair of original Derby-built vehicles, later given the numeric identity of Class 114, are seen near Ancaster on 28 May 1966. The train is the 17.52 Sleaford to Grantham, led by a DMB vehicle from the batch 50000-50049.* Michael Mensing

Right Below: *A Park Royal two-car set, led by its Driving Motor Brake passes near Bentley Heath Crossing, Knowle & Dorridge on 5 August 1966 forming the 17.00 Leamington Spa to Birmingham Snow Hill. When BR issued numeric classification to its DMU fleet, the Park Royal sets were classified as 103. For a short time the powered vehicles were 103 and the trailer cars Class 145, but this was soon changed to all vehicles of a set allocated the same classification.* Michael Mensing

Below: *A view which is somewhat different today. Recorded on 26 September 1966, we see a Metro-Cammell two-car set depart from Shildon in County Durham forming the 13.45 Bishop Auckland to Darlington. The leading vehicle is Driving Motor Brake 50200 which has an NE (North Eastern) prefix to its number. It is interesting to note that although of the same class, the cream body banding is different on each vehicle the DMB has cant rail and waist height bands, while the Driving Trailer has a solebar and mid-height band.* Michael Mensing

Above: *The route from London St Pancras to Bedford was 'modernised' in 1959 when a fleet of Derby-built four-car sets, later classified as 127 were introduced. These high-density sets provided an excellent service and remained in traffic until Class 317 'Bed-Pan' electrics were introduced in the early 1980s. On 20 June 1965, a four-car set is seen south of Ampthill Tunnel forming the 16.20 St Pancras to Bedford.* **Michael Mensing**

Below: *With Park Hall Halt in the background (provided to serve Park Hall hospital), a BR Derby-built two car set, led by Driving Trailer No. 56122 operates the 18.05 Gobowen to Oswestry service on Sunday 30 August 1964. This unit is another obvious case of where the original cream 'whiskers' have been replaced with a solid yellow warning panel, with a segment of the original 'whisker' still showing. It is interesting to note that a white edge has been given to the destination indicator, which for some reason has been wound round to display just a white screen. Under later BR classification this build of Derby vehicles were given the identity Class 108.* **Michael Mensing**

Above: *Some of the most popular DMMU vehicles were the dual-cab single vehicles frequently referred to as 'Bubble Cars'. Two manufacturers built this type of vehicle, Gloucester RC&W and Pressed Steel. Each builder also supplied a number of Driving Trailer vehicles to operate with the single cars to provide a two-car train. Both types of vehicle were high-density with doors by each seating bay. On 26 September 1959 a pair of 'Bubble Cars' Nos. W55004 and W55005 stand at Dudley Station after arriving with the 14.55 from Birmingham Snow Hill and prior to forming the 16.00 return service. With only a single car one problem with these vehicles was the positioning of the exhaust stacks, which had to pass up the bodywork at the cab end, this was positioned using small pipes which shadowed the window frames and originally terminated in an exhaust box above the destination indicator, later these were modified to vent directly.* **Michael Mensing**

Below: *Taking the Berkswell direct line at Kenilworth Junction, the 07.59 Leamington Spa to Birmingham New Street was recorded on 25 June 1964 formed of a pair of Birmingham RC&W and Metro Cammell two-car sets. The leading vehicle is No. 50539, a Driving Motor Brake.* **Michael Mensing**

Preservation Masterclass

Preservation of modern traction railway locomotives and multiple units is now big business in the UK. In the early 1970s when some of the most significant classes were withdrawn and broken up, the vast majority of enthusiasts who had cash to spare to devote to such projects were only interested in securing the long term future of steam traction.

One of the earliest attempts at modern traction preservation was by Colin Massingham and latterly the Diesel Traction Group who tried to save a D6300 class from the cutters torch and were later successful in purchasing Class 42 'Warship' No. D821 *Greyhound*.

Little did anyone at the time appreciate that this was just the cracking of the door on diesel

and more recently electric preservation, with today several hundred examples, covering most main stream classes in the hands of preservation groups throughout the country.

The quality and level of restoration is frankly outstanding, when compared with similar ventures in other countries, with today most of the 'larger' preserved lines having several preserved main line diesel locomotives in 'show-room' condition, representing liveries and modifications covering the entire lives of most classes.

The technical challenges of restoring a sophisticated item of machinery would put most people off and the sheer cost of procuring major items such as generators, fuel injectors, batteries

and turbo-charges or even complete power units could be a daunting task.

However, today we see a superb selection of fully operational main line diesel locomotives, several of which are now Network Rail main line certified, enabling younger enthusiasts to enjoy the sights and sounds of the earlier diesel classes.

Full credit must be given to the dedicated bands of preservationists throughout the country.

In the next six pages we look at just a small selection of masterpieces in modern traction preservation, in no way can we show examples from all groups or all classes, but we have tried to select a cross selection of preservation projects. ∎

Class 37/0 No. 37037 is owned by The Devon Diesel Society and is usually kept on the South Devon Railway. The locomotive was purchased from Barrow Hill in scrap condition in mid-2004 and arrived on the Devon line in June 2004. Thousands of man hours later and the loco was restored to fully operational condition and originally restored to BR rail blue with full yellow ends. In 2008 the loco was restored to 1960s all-over BR green, complete with buffer beam skirts and its original number D6737. The loco was hauled by rail from The South Devon Railway to The West Somerset Railway for its June 2008 Diesel Gala and was one of the highlights of the show, operating the full length of the 21 mile preserved line several times during the weekend event. Resplendent in BR green without a yellow warning end, No. D6737 approaches Doniford Halt on 14 June 2008 powering a service from Minehead to Bishops Lydeard. CJM

Above: *A locomotive which was returned to traffic in full 1980s rail blue in 2009 was No. 37109, a privately-owned loco which is kept on the East Lancs Railway. On 30 May 2009, it is seen approaching Burrs powering the 14.20 Heywood to Rawtenstall formed of four matching 1980s-liveried blue/grey Mk1 passenger coaches, faithfully reproducing a scene seen thousands of times on our network in the past years.* **Richard Hargreaves**

Below: *Another rail blue preserved example is No. 37075, owned by the 5C Loco Group and kept on the Churnet Valley Railway. This example has yellow route boxes, a white cant rail band and a Kingfisher logo on the bodyside. On 1 June 2009, it is seen emerging from the 531 yard Leebrook Tunnel powering the Churnet Valley Railway's breakdown train during an East Midlands Railway Photographic Society's photo charter, on what can only be described as a glorious day.* **Chris Perkins**

Above: *Former Freightliner Class 47 No. 47270 is now privately owned and operated on the Nene Valley Railway. The locomotive has been superbly restored to 1970s BR rail blue with an operational four-character route indicator and named in traditional style with the plates Swift. On 23 February 2008 the loco was chartered by the East Midlands Railway Photographic Society for a night time photo shoot at Wansford station, where it was posed with a period freight train.* **Chris Perkins**

Below: *The Class 14 'Teddy Bear' 0-6-0 diesel-hydraulic Type 1 locos are very popular with enthusiasts and a number are preserved. Here Nos. D9520 from the Nene Valley Railway and D9526 from the West Somerset Railway, are seen near Stogumber on the West Somerset line on 16 June 2008 powering the 10.05 Minehead to Bishops Lydeard. Both locos are sporting original 1960s style two-tone green with yellow/black 'wasp' ends.* **CJM**

Above: *In what can only be described as a masterpiece in both preservation and photography, is this line up at Barrow Hill Round House on 3 October 2003, of National Railway Museum preserved diesel locomotives English Electric prototype 'Deltic', Type 4 No. D200 and Type 1 No. D8000. These three locos are more usually to be found at either the main National Railway Museum site in York, or the Locomotion display at Shildon.* **Phil Wright**

Below: *Four Class 24s were saved by the preservation movement, with in late 2009 three fully operational. The picturesque Gloucester & Warwickshire Railway is home for privately-owned No. 24081, which is restored in BR rail blue colours. On 21 October 2007 the loco is seen exiting Greet Tunnel and approaching Winchcombe with a passenger service from Cheltenham Racecourse bound for Toddington.* **Jack Boskett**